Everything You Need to Know About

ASTHMA

Ten percent of children in the United States suffer from asthma. It's a serious, but treatable, condition.

Everything You Need to Know About

ASTHMA

Carolyn Simpson

THE ROSEN PUBLISHING GROUP, INC.
NEW YORK

Published in 1998 by The Rosen Publishing Group, Inc.
29 East 21st Street, New York, NY 10010

First Edition

Library of Congress Cataloging-in-Publication Data

Simpson, Carolyn.
    Everything you need to know about asthma / Carolyn Simpson
        p.   cm. -- (The need to know library)
    Includes bibliographical references and index.
    Summary: Explains what asthma is, how it is diagnosed and treated, and how
it can affect a person's life.
    ISBN 0-8239-2567-6
    1. Asthma--Juvenile literature. [1. Asthma]   I. Title.
  II. Series.
  RC591.S335   1998
  616.2'38--dc21   98-10118
                                                    CIP
                                                       AC

Manufactured in the United States of America

Contents

Introduction

*T*he day was unusually cold for October. Kids could see their breath as they stood outside waiting for their bus. Shandra wrapped her scarf around her neck and pulled it up to cover her mouth.

David came up behind her and tugged on the scarf. "Hey Shandra, you look like a snowman."

Shandra grabbed the scarf and pulled it back over her mouth. "I have asthma," she explained.

"Oh, I didn't know that," David said. "Is wearing a scarf some new kind of treatment?"

"I guess in a way. Cold air can give me an asthma attack. When I breathe through a scarf, the air becomes a little warmer."

"What's an asthma attack like?" David asked.

"I can't breathe," she said. "I start coughing, but it feels as if someone is squeezing my chest."

"Sounds pretty bad," David said.

"Well, it's scary, but I have my trusty inhaler with me. I'd rather not have the attack in the first place, though. Which is why I look like a snowman right now."

Suffering an asthma attack in cold, windy weather is not unusual. It illustrates two important points about asthma: While asthma can be a frightening, even life-threatening condition, it is manageable with proper medication and preventive measures.

In this book, you'll learn what asthma is and how common it is. Ten percent of all children in the United States suffer from this condition. Most people with asthma develop it during childhood. Some do eventually outgrow the condition, but others do not. You'll also learn that asthma is not "all in your head," although your emotions can certainly make the symptoms harder to treat. This book will also discuss the various medications (including pills, breathing treatments, and inhalers) used to treat asthma and the dangers of treating yourself with over-the-counter (OTC) remedies. Between 10 to 15 million people in the United States seek medical treatment for their asthma symptoms. Another 10 million people use OTC remedies.

Finally, you will learn how asthma can change your life and the lives of those around you. You need to adapt to your school's rules about carrying your medication; find sports and other activities that don't trigger your asthma attacks; and deal with all the feelings you have

Cold, windy weather can cause some people to have an asthma attack.

toward your family and friends who do not have this condition.

People are diagnosed with asthma at every stage of life. Infants are diagnosed with asthma and require special attention (and medication) early in their lives. Sometimes teenagers are diagnosed with asthma after engaging in sports or other activities that require strenuous physical activity. Sometimes people aren't diagnosed with asthma until they are in their fifties and sixties, and they suddenly start having allergies to things in their environment. Sometimes children who suffer greatly from asthma as infants appear to outgrow the condition. They don't require asthma medication until later in their lives when the asthma suddenly resurfaces.

No matter when the asthma is diagnosed, it's always treatable. Some cases are harder to treat than others, but with proper care and treatment, asthma can be managed, and the individual can live a long and healthy life.

Although asthma is a chronic condition, it comes and goes. An asthma attack affects a person's ability to breathe.

Chapter 1

What Is Asthma?

Asthma is a chronic condition that affects the lungs and the ability to breathe. Unlike other lung conditions, asthma comes and goes. People have asthma attacks and then recover. For periods of time, they are fine, then they suffer another attack.

Asthma affects the lungs, specifically the bronchial tubes. Think of a person's airways as an upside-down tree. The windpipe (called the trachea) represents the trunk of the tree. The bronchial tubes that extend into the right and left lungs represent the tree's largest branches. The bronchioles are the smaller tubes that branch off the bronchial tubes, like smaller branches in a tree. The alveoli, like leaves on a branch, are the small part of the respiratory system. Surrounding the alveoli are millions of tiny blood vessels. They take the oxygen that someone breathes in from the alveoli and add it to the blood. This oxygenated blood is pumped back into the heart and then distributed throughout the rest of the body. At the same time, the tiny blood vessels exchange the used air (carbon dioxide) in the blood and that is breathed out. A person wouldn't be able to survive long if he or she couldn't get rid of the toxic carbon dioxide in his or her blood.

The Trachea

The trachea is the long tube, commonly called the windpipe, that extends from the back of the throat to the entrance to the lungs. It's made up of bands of muscle. Muscle can do two things: tighten (constrict) or relax and open up (dilate). Ordinarily, when a person takes a breath, the air is taken in through the mouth or nose and travels down the windpipe to the bronchial tubes. Eventually the oxygen that is breathed in is added to the blood. If a person has asthma, the trachea and bronchial tubes are overly sensitive. When they are irritated, the muscles and the lining constrict more easily.

The Asthma Attack

There are a number of things that can trigger an asthma attack. Most of these triggers, however, are probably allergies that the asthmatic person has. When a person is allergic to a substance and it enters the body, the bronchioles can sometimes overact. Muscles in the lung airways swell up, and the production of mucus increases. The result is that the flow of air into and out

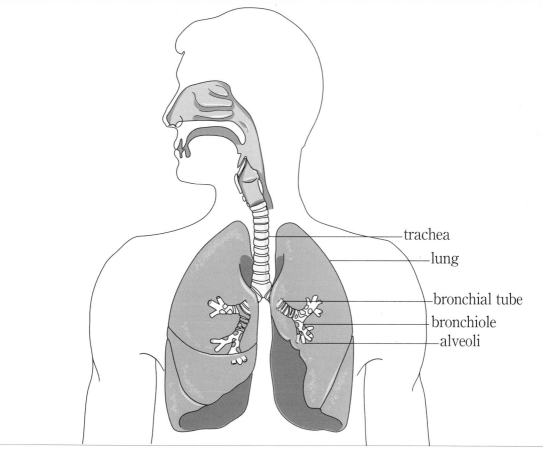

During an asthma attack, the airflow from the trachea and bronchial tubes to the lungs is restricted, making it hard to breathe.

of the lungs is decreased or is completely blocked. To many people, it feels as if an invisible hand is squeezing tightly their windpipe or chest. They can only gasp for air.

Grant dribbled down the basketball court at full speed. He weaved in and around the other players until he found the perfect shot. He jumped; the ball soared, circled the basket's rim, and finally sank through the net. The crowd cheered, but Grant was doubled over, desperately trying to breathe. The coach heard him wheezing and called for a time-out.

"Get his inhaler," the coach yelled to one of the other players.

He pulled Grant into a standing position and told him to calm down—his inhaler was on the way. "Don't breathe so hard," he advised. "Slow down. You're hyperventilating."

Asthma attacks are as different as the people who have them. Some people do more wheezing than coughing. Others breathe so fast and so shallowly that their fingers and toes get tingly because they aren't receiving enough oxygen. Some people start laughing and end up coughing and choking. There are also people who panic because they feel as if someone has thrown a blanket over their head, and they can't get enough fresh air. If you've experienced the following symptoms on more than one occasion, it's important that you see your doctor. A doctor will be able to diagnose asthma. Only then will you be able to receive proper treatment.

- Wheezing, when breathing produces a whistling sound
- Coughing episodes, often preceded by laughing or crying
- Difficulty breathing that goes away after thirty or forty minutes
- A tightening sensation in the chest, as if someone were sitting on you
- The sensation of being under a blanket and not getting enough fresh air
- Tingling in fingers and toes from hyperventilation

- Difficulty breathing after six or eight minutes of hard exercise
- Avoidance of aerobic activities because you're always short of breath

We've discussed what asthma is and how asthma physically affects the body. Asthma is a very real condition that affects many people, but you may wonder why some people develop it and others don't. In the next chapter we will discuss what causes some people to develop asthma.

Chapter 2

How Do You Get Asthma?

Although scientists still don't know all the answers to what causes asthma or why someone develops asthma, they do know that asthma is most likely an inherited condition. While they have yet to discover an asthma gene, they still suspect that a gene is responsible. That may explain why children born into families with a history of asthma have a greater likelihood of developing asthma themselves.

The Immune System and Asthma

The immune system plays a big role in the development of asthma. The immune system protects the body from foreign invaders, such as viruses, bacteria, and other germs, which can potentially harm the body. When the body detects an invader, it produces two types of cells to combat this invader: B cells and T cells. T cells attack the invader directly. B cells, on the other hand, produce antibodies that circulate in the bloodstream looking for invaders to destroy. An invader that causes the body to develop antibodies against it is called an antigen. The B cells produce five kinds of antibodies, which are composed of a protein called immunoglobulin. Immunoglobulin E (IgE) is the antibody that is most involved in allergic reactions.

The immune system operates efficiently to protect the body from harmful substances, but sometimes, for unknown reasons, the body reacts to harmless substances that enter the body. This reaction is known as an allergy.

Scientists believe some people develop asthma because of allergic reactions to harmless substances, such as pollen, mold spores, certain types of food, and animal dander. Although these substances in themselves pose no threat to the average person, they can cause an allergic person to have a reaction, such as an asthma attack.

Histamine

When an allergen (an antigen that stimulates the body to produce antibodies) enters the body, it reacts with the antibody IgE. IgE is found on the surface of circulating white blood cells called basophils and on mast cells (a type of cell that lines the walls of the nose, bronchial tubes, intestines, and skin). The basophils and mast cells react to the allergen by releasing histamine, a chemical that can irritate the body, and other harmful

Something as common as air freshener spray can cause an attack in someone who has asthma.

chemicals to fight off the invader. When histamine is released, it causes the surrounding tissues to become inflamed and swollen.

When it is released in the lungs, histamine causes a number of reactions similar to those of an asthma attack. It causes the secretion of mucus in the lungs, and the linings of airways narrow and swell up. This eventually leads to wheezing, breathlessness, and coughing.

While allergic reactions are one possible cause for the development of asthma, scientists are still trying to discover other possible causes.

Common Allergens

Jodie started getting a headache one afternoon during her

sixth-hour history class. When the bell rang, and students opened the door to the hall, the strong odor of insecticide filled the room. Someone was spraying for cockroaches in the hallway.

Jodie started to cough. Before she knew it, she was gasping for air. She reached for her inhaler. The fumes of the insecticide had brought on an asthma attack.

People with asthma have bronchial tubes that are far more sensitive to irritants in the air than people who don't have asthma. When a person with asthma comes in contact with an allergen, histamine is released, setting off the asthma reaction. Common allergens include mold, dust, cockroaches, and tobacco smoke. Many people are also allergic to the saliva, urine, and dander (dead skin cells) of cats.

Mold and Dust

Mold is more than the green stuff you see on aging bread and cheese. It's present in house plants, in shower stalls and on curtains, and in humidifiers. Many people are allergic to microscopic molds. These are molds that cannot be seen by the naked eye.

Dust is another powerful allergen and one that's very hard to eliminate. Dust is made up of some unpleasant ingredients: mold, pollen, food particles, mite and cockroach feces and body parts, animal dander, and dead human skin cells. A person can be allergic to any one of these ingredients. Scientists believe that the rise in asthma cases among inner-city youths is because cockroaches are so common in inner-city apartment dwellings.

Pets

Pets can also be powerful allergens. The dander of animals floats around in the air. Cat dander is the smallest and strongest airborne allergen. Its effects linger long after the pet has gone. This is why putting the cat in another room doesn't help those who are allergic to it. Although the cat isn't in the room, its dander is all over the house. Cat dander stays in a place for a long time. The allergic person will continue to have a reaction to it.

Smoke

Tobacco smoke and smoke from a wood-burning stove can be very toxic to some people. In this case, the allergen is smoke. Smoke triggers the production of histamine and causes inflammation in the surrounding tissues. The individual who's allergic to smoke doesn't have to be the one smoking. Second-hand smoke (what you breathe in when other people are smoking around you) is just as toxic to the asthmatic who's allergic to smoke.

Food Allergies

Sometimes food allergies provoke an asthma attack. Food allergies are often the most frightening. When people eat something and have an allergic reaction, they

Cat dander, saliva, and urine are common allergens that can trigger an attack of allergies or asthma.

risk having their throats close up in a matter of minutes. Common food allergens are nuts, milk products, and shellfish.

Infections

Infections, especially in the respiratory system, can also contribute to the development of asthma attacks. Often people with asthma wind up in the hospital following a viral infection because their asthma, coupled with the virus, became harder to control.

Exercise-Induced Asthma

Finally, some people develop asthma symptoms in certain weather conditions (either hot and humid air, smog, or on cold and windy days) or after playing certain strenuous sports. Sports that involve a lot of running, such as track or soccer, are harder on the person with asthma. After six or eight minutes of hard exercise, a person prone to asthma attacks may suffer an attack. Other sports, such as softball or baseball, in which the running occurs in spurts, are less likely to bring on an asthma attack.

Chapter 3

How Is Asthma Diagnosed and Treated?

You need to see a doctor to diagnose asthma properly because asthma can be a difficult condition to identify. Many other conditions, such as bronchitis, pneumonia, cystic fibrosis, and even swallowing something that gets stuck in the throat, can look like asthma.

Asthma is commonly misdiagnosed. If possible, try to see a doctor who specializes in asthma. You can help your doctor by noting all your symptoms and when they occur. It's also important to find out if you have a family history of any respiratory disease or allergies. Have you ever suffered from respiratory infections, frequent ear infections, sinus congestion, or allergies? Is there a family history of bronchitis, asthma, or allergic reactions?

Conditions like asthma can run in families, although not always from generation to generation. Your grandmother may have it and a couple of your cousins may have it even if your own parents and siblings don't have it. Your family medical history is very important in helping the doctor diagnose your condition.

If you suspect you may have asthma, keep a list of your symptoms. Do you have breathing difficulties, and if so, when do they occur? Do they occur in the morning (when asthma symptoms are typically worst) or following hard exercise or in certain kinds of weather? Do your symptoms come and go, or are they constant, as if you have a terrible cold? Have you found yourself avoiding certain activities or certain environments because they make you short of breath? Keeping a record of when and where your attacks occur and how severe they are will help your doctor diagnose your condition. It will also help you figure out what environments and activities to avoid.

Tests to Diagnose Asthma

Unfortunately there aren't any definitive tests to diagnose asthma. Unless you're in the midst of an asthma attack, the doctor won't necessarily see signs of breathing difficulties. And you usually can't schedule an asthma attack for the date and time of your doctor's appointment. So how do doctors determine if you have asthma?

The physical exam may reveal little information beyond ruling out what you don't have. A chest X ray could detect pneumonia or a foreign body lodged in your throat, but it won't suggest asthma. If allergies are a suspected cause, the doctor can try to induce an asthma attack.

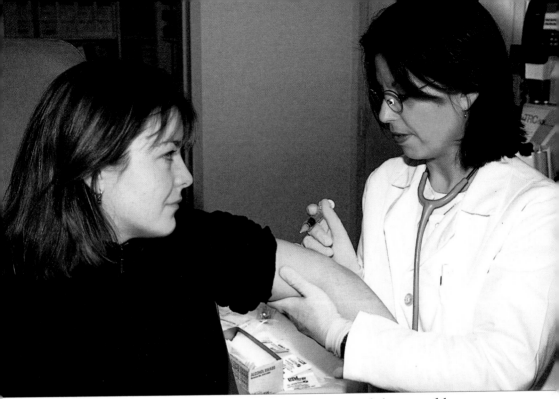

One test to determine whether an asthma attack is caused by an allergen is to inject the allergen into the patient.

One common method used to do this is to put a drop of allergen onto your skin and then prick your skin to let the allergen enter your body. If you're allergic to the allergen, you'll react. More serious skin tests involve scratching the skin and then putting drops of allergen over the scratched areas. Another method requires injecting the allergen directly under the skin. If the allergen provokes an asthma attack, and if a bronchodilating drug stops the asthma attack once it has started, the doctor can be fairly certain you have asthma.

Pulmonary Functioning Tests

Pulmonary functioning tests are helpful because they determine how much air the patient can breathe out,

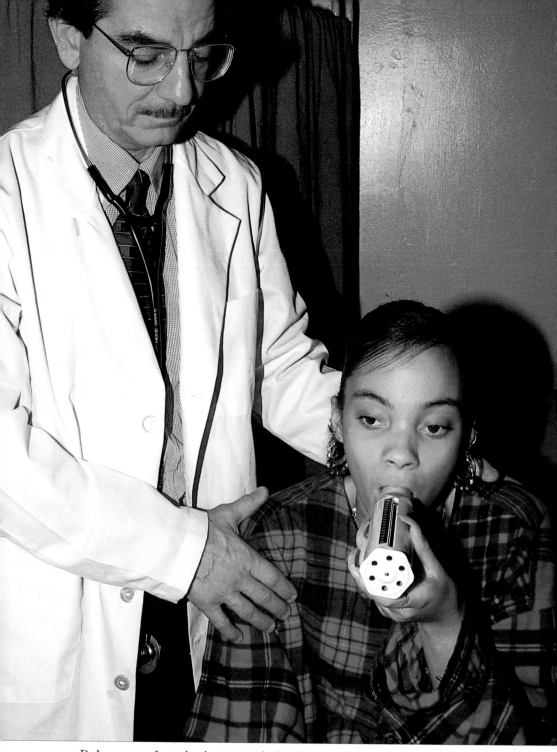

Pulmonary functioning tests help doctors determine a patient's lung capacity.

which indicates lung capacity. The patient is asked to breathe out as much air as possible into a tube that measures the force of the expulsion. Then if the patient is having breathing difficulties, the doctor gives a bronchodilating medication and allows ten to fifteen minutes for the medication to take effect. The doctor then asks the patient to breathe into the tube again. If the next effort produces at least a 20 percent increase in air expulsion, the patient is believed to have asthma because the medication reversed the symptoms of airway obstruction.

If the patient is breathing easily when he or she goes to the doctor, the doctor may try to provoke an asthma attack. The doctor may ask the patient to breathe from a neutral solution containing methacholine (or histamine). Methacholine will provoke breathing difficulties in an asthmatic. Sometimes the doctor will have the patient breathe in cold air or exercise for six to eight minutes to see if that brings on an asthma attack. If either of these methods cause a 20 percent reduction in the patient's lung capacity, it's a solid indication that the person has asthma.

Preventive Medications

There are two ways to treat asthma. One way is to take preventive action, controlling the production and inflammation of the bronchial tubes before an attack occurs. The other way is to treat the asthma attack in progress, dilating the bronchial tubes and helping the patient breathe again.

Theophylline

Theophylline is one of the older asthma medications; it relieves bronchial spasms by relaxing the smooth muscle of the airways and blood vessels in the lungs. Theophylline comes in a variety of pills. A short-acting pill, taken every four hours, has its maximum effect after two hours and leaves the body after four hours. The intermediate-acting pill is taken every eight hours (which may be more convenient); its peak effects occur after four hours, and it leaves the body after eight hours. Long-acting theophylline is taken once every twenty-four hours and may not reach its peak effects for two or three days.

Theophylline has to build up in your bloodstream in order to be effective. It's not something you take only when you're feeling bad. The only way doctors can determine if you have the correct amount in your bloodstream is to perform blood tests every so often. This helps them determine the exact level of the drug needed.

Smokers use up theophylline more quickly than non-smokers. Those using theophylline should also avoid products that contain large amounts of caffeine, such as tea, coffee, and cola. The biggest problem with theophylline is that the effective dose is close to the toxic dose. In other words, for theophylline to do its job, you have to take almost as much as the amount that would hurt you.

Some unpleasant side effects associated with theophylline include nausea, shakiness, stomach cramps, diarrhea, and vomiting. The more severe side effects may result from an accidental overdose. While a mild overdose can cause nausea and restlessness, a larger overdose can lead to serious heartbeat irregularities, convulsions, and even death. If you suspect an overdose, seek medical attention immediately.

Cromolyn Sodium

Another preventive drug for asthma is cromolyn sodium, marketed under the name Intal. It works to prevent the release of histamine but also works on the inflamed areas that occur with chronic asthma. The only drawback to cromolyn sodium is that it doesn't stop an asthma attack once it has started. Cromolyn sodium is used on a regular basis as a preventive method.

Bronchodilating Drugs

Adrenaline is used to open up the bronchial tubes in emergency situations. It's not routinely used because it also speeds up the heart rate and increases blood pressure. Some of the over-the-counter (OTC) drugs use a combination of adrenaline (epinephrine) and theophylline. However, to get the therapeutic dose of theophylline, you would have to take too much adrenaline (which would affect your heart).

Scientists have also discovered adrenaline-like medications. Terbutaline and albuterol are medications that don't affect the person's heart. The best thing about these medications is that they are inhaled. They provide relief that goes directly to the lungs and have fewer side effects. Oral medications have more side effects because they're swallowed, and they go through your system. Adrenaline-like medications are also called bronchodilators because they dilate the bronchial tubes. Some people use inhalers regularly to prevent problems. Others use them only when they fear an asthma attack or when an attack is happening. Brethaire, Ventolin, and Proventil are commonly prescribed bronchodilators.

The Federal Food and Drug Administration (FDA) recently approved a new class of drugs called Accolate. These drugs work by blocking the activities of certain molecules in the lungs that cause asthma symptoms.

Inhalers

Inhalers are convenient and fast acting, but they can cause problems for some people. People can overuse their inhalers. When you use your inhaler more often than it's supposed to be used, you're ignoring the warning signs of increasing asthma problems. You should consult your doctor. He or she may prescribe additional breathing treatments. Overuse of inhalers can have dangerous consequences. It can lead to an opposite effect: instead of dilating the bronchial tubes, they start constricting, or narrowing, the bronchial tubes.

How to Use Your Inhaler

Inhalers aren't always easy to use. The inhaler is a handheld device with a measured amount of medicine in each spray. You will always get the right dose of medicine, but you may have a hard time directing the medicine to

Some doctors believe that you should hold an inhaler firmly between your lips while you spray it.

where you want it to go. Spraying it all over your face or tongue does little to provide relief.

There are different types of inhalers available, so there are different ways to use them. You can ask your doctor or a nurse for help on how best to use your inhaler. There is no one specific method to use an inhaler. Some doctors recommend that you hold the inhaler two inches from your mouth to get the maximum amount of medication. Others tell you to hold it between your lips. If you have trouble using it this way, your doctor may recommend an easier method. The following are some simple instructions:

1. Always shake your inhaler well before using it.
2. Take a deep breath and then let it go slowly.

3. Hold the inhaler two inches from your mouth. Open your mouth.
4. Press down once to spray a dose in your mouth. The right amount of medicine will come out.
5. Breathe in slowly and deeply; then hold your breath for ten seconds.
6. Breathe out slowly afterward. The idea is to deliver as much of the medicine as possible deep into your bronchial tubes.

The Spacer

If you have trouble holding the inhaler two inches from your mouth and getting the medication in properly, you might ask your doctor to prescribe a spacer. A spacer costs around $20 and can only be purchased with a prescription.

The spacer greatly simplifies the job. It's a cylinder or tube that attaches directly to your inhaler. It keeps the inhaler two inches from your mouth, so you can put your lips directly over the mouthpiece, forming a seal.

The spacer makes the inhaler less convenient to carry around, which is its drawback. However, its advantage is that it's hard to make a mistake using a spacer. You just spray a dose and breathe in very slowly. If you inhale too quickly, the spacer will make a whistling sound, indicating that you didn't do it right. If you're supposed to spray twice, wait five minutes between each puff.

There are new kinds of equipment that don't require the user to put any distance between the inhaler and the mouth. Ask your doctor for more information.

Vivica made a long run down the soccer field, kicking the ball around defenders and drawing the goalie away from the goal. At the last minute she leaned back and fired the ball into the uppermost corner of the net. It went in.

"I need my inhaler," Vivica said, as she wheezed and tried to catch her breath. She headed for the sidelines.

The coach sent in a sub for Vivica and told her to catch her breath. Vivica reached into her bag and pulled out her inhaler. She shook it and sprayed. Nothing came out. She shook it and sprayed again. Again, nothing.

"It's empty," Vivica shouted, throwing the inhaler back into her bag. She was still breathing hard and furiously.

The coach came up to Vivica and threw her arm over Viv's shoulders. "Not a good time to be out of medicine, huh?" she said.

"Just walk around a little and try to relax. You'll be okay," her coach said, looking worried herself.

Vivica eventually stopped wheezing, but she spent the rest of the game on the sidelines.

Empty or Full?

You can't rely on outside markers to tell if your inhaler is full or near empty. The container is an aerosol can and the weight can be deceiving. However, there's an easy way to determine how much medication is left in your inhaler. Simply fill a big bowl with water. Make sure the cover is on your inhaler and then drop it carefully into the bowl of water. If the inhaler sinks to the bottom, it's

full. If it floats on the top, it's empty. The farther down
it sits in the water the more medication remains in the
inhaler. When it's halfway from the surface, it's time to
buy another inhaler. Don't discard the inhaler that's only
half full; keep using it, but keep a full one on hand for
when the other one runs out.

Serevent

Serevent is a new bronchodilating drug that lasts hours
longer than the previous ones. Whereas Ventolin would
begin working in ten or fifteen minutes and last three
or four hours, Serevent begins to work in thirty to forty
minutes and lasts up to twelve hours.

Because it takes so long to start working, it is not
meant to be used to stop an asthma attack in progress.
Again, it is a preventive measure. If you have an attack,
your old inhaler will provide quicker relief. Its effects
just won't last as long.

Most people who play sports and have exercise-
induced asthma rely on both types of medication.
Cromolyn sodium or Serevent can prevent most
attacks when taken prior to the exercise, but only
Ventolin or Proventil will help once an attack is under-
way.

Steroids for Chronic or Severe Asthma

Chronic asthma (a condition that bothers you over a
long period of time) or severe asthma may require more

One way to test if an inhaler is empty or full is to drop it into a large bowl of water. If it floats, it's empty; if it sinks, it's full.

medicine than bronchodilators and preventive drugs can provide. In these cases, the airways remain chronically inflamed and swollen.

Corticosteroids (a modified form of human hormones) are used to treat asthma because they help control inflammation and mucus production. These are the two things that make an asthma attack more dangerous. When the mast cells release histamine, white blood cells rush into the area. They increase the inflammation. Cortisone (and derivatives) lower the number of white blood cells drawn to the area. Fewer white cells means less inflammation.

Corticosteroids come in several forms: tablets, injections, inhaled medications, and nasal sprays. The use of all corticosteroids needs to be reduced gradually under a doctor's supervision, not suddenly stopped. It takes the body time to adjust to increases and decreases in hormone levels.

Allergy Shots

Since asthma can be triggered by allergies, some people take allergy shots (or immunotherapy) to lessen their sensitivity to allergens. The allergy shots encourage the body to produce more T cells, which will suppress IgE antibody production.

Some patients get allergy shots (which are small amounts of the allergen) once a week in the doctor's office. The nurse usually gives the shot, and you wait around for about half an hour to be sure you aren't going to suffer any allergic reaction.

If you do have a bad reaction, the nurse has adrenaline on hand to give you to counteract the allergen's effects. In that case, the doctor would have you continue with the shots but in smaller doses. The idea is to work up to the largest amount of allergen that won't cause a reaction.

Weekly shots eventually become bimonthly shots, and then monthly. Some people are able to stop taking allergy shots after a couple of years if they haven't had asthma attacks. Others need to take these shots all their lives. Allergy shots won't necessarily make your asthma go away, but they can reduce the amount of asthma medication needed to control symptoms.

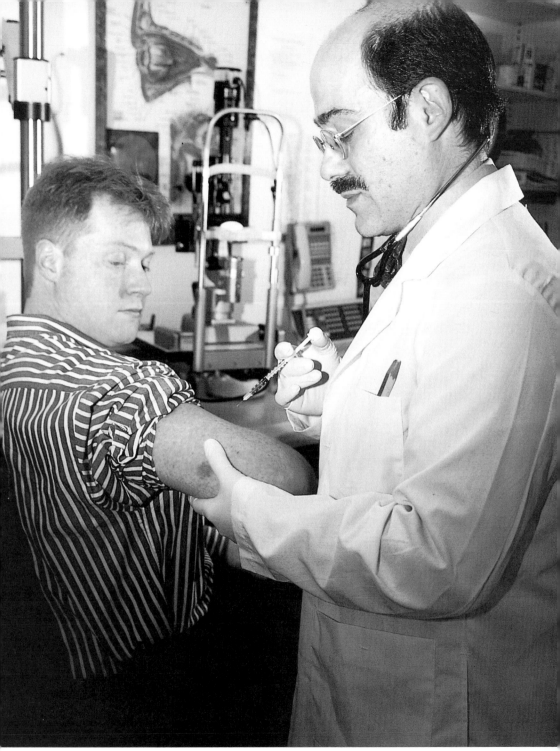

Allergy shots can help people build resistance to the substances they are allergic to.

The Dangers of Over-the-Counter Drugs

Model Krissy Taylor, sister of model Nikki Taylor, died of an asthma attack because she never knew she had asthma. She suffered from shortness of breath. Although she saw her doctor, he thought her symptoms were the result of bronchitis and a sore throat, not asthma. Krissy Taylor treated her symptoms with an over-the-counter (OTC) drug, which didn't treat her condition, but rather masked her symptoms. She had also unknowingly made her condition worse by smoking. If her asthma had been properly diagnosed and treated, she might still be alive today.

At drugstores, you may have seen several products that supposedly treat asthma and asthma-like symptoms. You can buy them without a prescription. If you want to avoid a costly doctor's prescription, you might think these OTC remedies are a good option. However, treating asthma or symptoms of asthma with OTC drugs and without a doctor's advice can have deadly consequences.

The problem with using OTC drugs is that they have fixed amounts of certain ingredients. In order to get enough of one ingredient, you may be getting an overdose of another ingredient. If you're not being treated by a doctor, you have no way of knowing if your condition is getting worse, until it's too late.

A doctor needs to diagnose and treat asthma. Your family doctor can treat uncomplicated asthma, but he or she may not know much about the latest medications used in treating asthma. You may see a pulmonary internist (a lung diseases specialist) or an allergist, depending on the suspected cause of your asthma.

Other Treatments

Antihistamines work well for people who have sinus problems, but they have little effect on asthma sufferers. In fact, sometimes antihistamines can dry out the asthmatic's bronchial tubes too much. This makes it less likely that the person can cough up any accumulating mucus. Stay away from OTC antihistamines unless they are recommended by your doctor.

Nebulizers

Nebulizers are machines that resemble humidifiers or vaporizers. They dispense medicine in the form of a fine mist. A person can breathe in the mist using a mask, a tube, or a mouthpiece. Nebulizers are helpful in getting medication quickly into your lungs. They're also easier to use than inhalers, but you need training to use them properly. If your doctor recommends that you use a nebulizer, he or she or a nurse can usually train you how to use it properly.

Postural Drainage

For people who are mostly bothered by mucus plugs, a procedure called postural drainage can be helpful. Someone pounds on the asthmatic's back. This dislodges

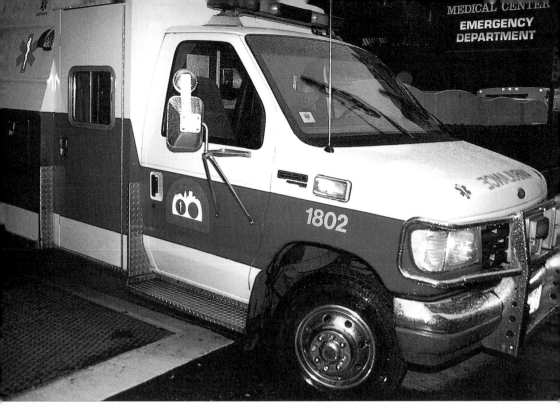

You may require emergency care if your airway becomes constricted and normal medications do not help.

mucus plugs from the trachea or bronchial tubes. It's important to realize that a person needs to be trained to use this procedure properly.

Peak Flow Meters

Peak flow meters look a little like spacers with a needle on the outside. They're tubes that you blow into several times a day to test your lung efficiency. You should be able to exhale forcefully (80 to 100 percent of your lung capacity) to be in the green zone. If the meter registers between 50 to 80 percent, you are in the yellow or cautionary zone. However, if you're in the red zone (50 percent or below), you're in the danger zone. This often means you're close to having an asthma attack. Use a bronchodilator and blow into the meter after the medicine has taken effect. If you're still in the red zone, contact your doctor immediately.

If you get into the habit of checking yourself everyday, you will know your asthma condition is worsening long before you have an attack. The peak flow meter is only used to show how well or poorly you're breathing at any given moment.

Emergency Room Treatment

Max woke up with an asthma attack. He grabbed his inhaler and took two puffs. Relief didn't come right away. Either a mucus plug was keeping the medication from reaching his bronchial tubes, or his airway obstruction was in the finer bronchioles that aren't so easily helped by the spray.

Max began to panic. He woke his parents up and told them the medicine wasn't working.

Seeing Max's distress, his parents tried to calm him down, but he was beginning to turn blue from lack of oxygen. They drove him to the nearby emergency room.

At the emergency room, Max was immediately put in a treatment room. Anyone who is having trouble breathing is considered a priority case and is treated immediately. First, a nurse gave Max a shot of adrenaline. Once the shot started to work on the blockage, the nurse began a breathing treatment to help break up the rest of his blockage. Within an hour, Max was ready to go back home.

Adrenaline shots are reserved for emergency treatment. That's because they are short acting and have a direct effect on the person's heart. When shots don't result in better breathing, doctors may recommend breathing treatments or bronchodilating drugs.

Status Asthmaticus

Status asthmaticus is the scariest condition an asthmatic can have. It means the situation is life-threatening. Your airway is constricted (and isn't responding to medication); you may be producing too much mucus that is clogging your bronchial tubes, and the walls of your bronchial tubes are probably inflamed and swollen (further narrowing the opening to breathe).

You will be admitted to the hospital. Don't panic! Even if adrenaline shots fail to work, there are other treatments that the doctor will consider. Sometimes nurses will start bronchial suctioning to try to suck out the excess mucus. If breathing is very difficult, and you're not getting enough oxygen into your blood, the doctor may put you on a respirator. The nurse will insert a respirator tube through your nose or mouth down into your trachea. Then it's attached to a breathing machine that will automatically inflate and deflate your lungs for you. You'll probably be taken off the respirator within twenty-four hours because doctors want you to breathe on your own as soon as possible.

The emergency room is supposed to be used when all else fails. Unfortunately, many people who can't afford regular doctor appointments or asthma medicine rely on the emergency room as their only means of treatment. Asthma is harder to manage when you're not taking preventive steps to treat it.

Chapter 4

How Will Asthma Affect Your Life?

*J*eremy's girlfriend, Rachel, had invited him over to her house for dinner. Her parents were eager to meet him, she had said.

Imagine Jeremy's surprise when he finally met Rachel's parents. Both were smoking cigarettes. Being asthmatic, Jeremy stood in the doorway wondering how to get through this evening. Tobacco smoke always set off an asthma attack for him. He knew he wouldn't be able to eat dinner in the house.

"Come on in," Mr. Dixon said. He pointed to a comfortable chair in the family room.

Jeremy could feel himself ready to cough. His nose had already clogged up; he knew his lungs were next. And he didn't have his inhaler with him.

"I'd really like to spend this evening with you. Here, I brought you flowers," he said to Mrs. Dixon. "But I have

Being around people who smoke may increase the number of asthma attacks you have.

to tell you that I have asthma, and I'm allergic to smoke." Jeremy stood there looking embarrassed.

At that point he started to wheeze. Mr. and Mrs. Dixon crushed their cigarettes in the ashtray.

"Hey, look. No problem," Mr. Dixon said, jumping up. "We can go out for dinner. We can pick a nonsmoking place."

Jeremy felt more embarrassed to have caused this change of plans. However, he was having trouble breathing and just nodded. Stepping into the fresh air relieved his cough, but he know he'd still have to stop by his house to get his inhaler.

"I should have thought to bring my inhaler," he told Rachel.

"I should have told you they smoked," Rachel said. "I never knew you were so allergic."

"No harm done," Mr. Dixon said. "We'll stop by your house, then we can try out that new restaurant in town."

Asthma can force some changes in your life. There will be some places you'll have to avoid and some activities you'll have to learn to deal with. What if Jeremy had wanted to go dancing with Rachel later that evening? Where would they have gone? Clubs are usually smoky places, and dancing is an aerobic activity. Both situations have the potential to provoke an asthma attack.

However, if Jeremy really wanted to take Rachel dancing, he could have found ways to adapt to his asthma. First, he could have used his inhaler, as he would before any physical activity. He could have danced some of the dances, but sat down when he was tired or had trouble breathing. Of course, he would have to pick a place that was relatively smoke-free, since secondhand smoke can set off his asthma. However, using his inhaler ahead of time might have lessened his airway sensitivity.

Asthma can affect every aspect of your life. Some activities should be avoided, but you can adapt to many others. Just because you have asthma doesn't mean that you can't have fun and do normal things just like everyone else. Don't think of asthma as something that can prevent you from living your life.

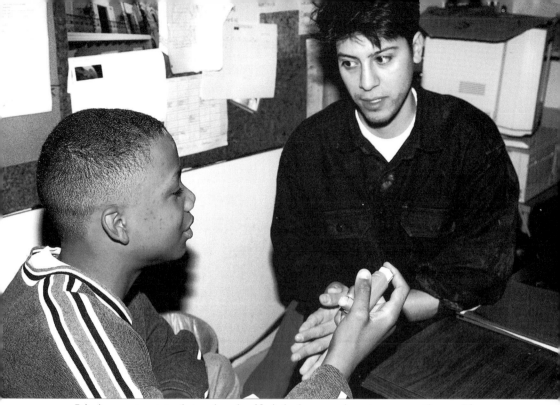

It's important to let school officials know about your asthma. If you have an attack, they will know how to help.

School

Many people with asthma try to keep their condition a secret. Perhaps they're afraid others won't understand what's wrong and will laugh at them if they have an attack. However, keeping your condition a secret isn't a good idea because it can prevent people from knowing what to do to help you if you have an attack. It's smarter to alert your teachers ahead of time and let your class-mates and friends know about your asthma. If you think of asthma as a physical condition, you'll be less likely to view it as a personal weakness.

Once asthma is diagnosed, you'll need to inform your school nurse and your teachers. In some schools, the nurse expects to hold your asthma medicine and give it to you when it's needed. In other schools, your parents can sign an agreement with the school nurse to let you carry your own medicine and use it when you feel the need. It's better to carry your medicine with you. Sometimes people don't have time to ask permission to go to the nurse's office to get their inhaler. If your school's policy is that the nurse must keep your medicine, ask your parents to talk with the school and make an exception in your case. Ask your doctor to write a note explaining that you need to carry your inhaler at all times in case of an attack. Sometimes school officials are swayed by doctor's notes and responsible students.

Whether or not you can carry your own medicine, you need to tell all your teachers about your condition. If you need to go to the nurse, you'll want teachers to know ahead of time that this is a possibility. If you carry your inhaler, talk to your teacher about what's the most convenient, least distracting way to use it during class. Some teachers prefer that you step out in the hall when you use your inhaler. Some would rather you went to the bathroom to use it. Others won't mind if you use it in the classroom.

If you suffer from exercise-induced asthma, be sure to tell your gym teacher ahead of time. Some weather conditions may prevent you from participating outside. Some activities may be off-limits to you as well. Decide ahead of time what you'll do in the event you can't participate on some days. A note from your doctor explaining the situation may be necessay.

Sports

Some activities will be easier to manage than others. Sports in which you're constantly running are more difficult to play. Soccer and long-distance running are tougher on the asthmatic than baseball and volleyball because the running is more constant. However, a great number of soccer players have asthma and play with the help of their inhalers.

Singing can be difficult if your lung capacity is reduced. However, aerobic activity can help strengthen your lung capacity if you take it slowly. Tae kwon do, a form of martial arts, is an excellent activity to help develop lung capacity and confidence.

Avoiding Asthma Triggers

If you're allergic to certain things, speak with your doctor about allergy shots. Also, try to reduce your exposure to allergens. You can also try to avoid situations where you're likely to come in contact with an allergen. Avoid asthma triggers when you can, and use preventive medication to help you tolerate those you can't avoid.

Dust

If you're allergic to dust, you might consider allergy shots, since dust is impossible to remove from your environment completely. When someone dusts in your home, ask him or her to use a furniture polish or a wet cloth because those items are able to collect and contain the dust. In fact, you shouldn't be present when the dusting and vacuuming are being done.

Cats

If you're allergic to cats, avoid going to the home of someone who has a cat. If you own a cat, consider finding a new home for your cat. If that sounds impossible, you can confine your cat outdoors depending on the weather. Keep the cat away from areas where you will spend lots of time, such as your room. As long as the cat is around, your asthma will be that much harder to treat.

Mold

If you're allergic to mold, you won't want to keep a lot of houseplants around, as they're breeding grounds for molds. Wash your curtains frequently and clean your vaporizer after each night's use. Molds grow in moist environments. If you live in a city with a high mold count, listen to the radio for mold count reports. Stay inside on days when mold counts are high.

Smoke

If you're allergic to smoke, don't smoke. Smoking further irritates your bronchial tubes and causes you to take more medication to help control your asthma attacks. Watch out for secondhand smoke, too. The smoke that others breathe out is just as damaging to your lungs and will cause bronchial spasms. Avoid

If you have exercise-induced asthma, it's important to know
what activities you can participate in and what activities you
should avoid.

places where there's smoke. Mention to smokers that you have asthma and are allergic to smoke. If they understand why you object to their smoking, they might be more likely to accommodate you.

Family and Feelings

Asthma doesn't just affect individuals; it affects whole families.

Julie was a severe asthmatic who frequently had to go to the emergency room. Because Julie was allergic to molds and lived in a town with a high mold count, her parents decided to move the family to a drier climate out West. Julie was thirteen at the time. She was forced to leave all her friends and begin seventh grade in an entirely new school. She was angry about the move but also felt guilty because her asthma was the reason they moved.

The rest of the family wasn't happy about the move either. Julie's father had to accept a job that paid him less; her older sister was two years from graduating high school and blamed Julie for disrupting her life. Julie's mother was overly protective and never let her do any-thing. She didn't allow Julie to go to parties or hang out with her friends. She was always worried that Julie would have an asthma attack.

"This is no way to live," Julie told a friend. "Everyone had to move and change their lives because of me. I feel guilty and angry."

"Why don't you try to tough it out?" her friend asked.

"I wish I could, but it's not so easy" Julie said. "Sometimes when I can't breathe, I get so scared. I think I could die, and I panic. It's a horrible feeling. It's only later that I start feeling sorry for myself. I just wish I could outgrow this."

If you have asthma, you probably have mixed feelings about your condition. You might feel angry that your activities are limited. You might feel guilty for taking so much of the family's attention, or you might feel scared at times when you can't breathe. Your brothers and sisters may have feelings about your asthma too. Perhaps they feel angry because you're the center of attention. They may also feel guilty because they get to do things that you can't do. Maybe they're scared that you could die during one of your asthma attacks.

You can't help having feelings about your condition. What you can do is acknowledge them and try to do something positive to help yourself. Read all you can about asthma and follow your doctor's treatment suggestions. The biggest complication for asthma sufferers is noncompliance, or not following the doctor's directions. Some people just don't like the idea of having asthma, so they act as if they don't have it. Denying your condition will make it that much harder to treat.

When you're feeling guilty or angry, share your feelings with your family. Chances are they're trying to cope with similar feelings. Once you discuss these openly, you can find ways to support each other. Pretending that your asthma doesn't affect the rest of your family only makes it harder for everyone to get along.

As you can see, asthma can affect many parts of your life as well as the lives of your family and friends. But millions of people have asthma, and they are all able to live normal and happy lives. Don't let asthma stop you from living your life.

Chapter 5

A Look into the Future

At this point in time, there is no cure for asthma, only ways to manage the condition. Current medications are aimed at preventing an asthma attack or stopping it once it has occurred.

The U.S. government is very cautious about approving new drugs to be sold to the public. The Food and Drug Administration has developed strict rules about the length of time a drug must be tested before it is approved. As a result, Europe and Canada and some other countries are able to use drugs before they are available in the United States. Nonetheless, new drugs are always being developed and tested.

Scientists are also hoping to find the asthma gene they suspect exists. If they do, they can use gene therapy to replace the defective gene. If that ever happens, it can lead to a cure for asthma.

Asthma can be a lifelong condition. Learn as much about it as you can. This knowledge can help you better deal with the problems that asthma can cause.

In the meantime, research the current information available. Learn all you can about the current medications available. Make sure you follow your doctor's orders. Reduce your exposure to allergens. Take your medicine as prescribed and in the amounts prescribed. Consult your doctor if you experience side effects.

Never stop taking a medication prescribed by your doctor without consulting him or her first. Also, never take medication without consulting with your doctor first, even if you find the medication in a drugstore and think it is safe. This medication may be dangerous for you. It can cause a dangerous interaction when combined with the medication given by your doctor.

Monitor your asthma symptoms carefully so you have a clearer idea of what causes your symptoms to worsen. It might be helpful to keep a journal of the day you experience an asthma attack. Write down what you were doing or where you were before the attack occurred. This way you will know what activities, things, or places you should avoid in order to prevent an asthma attack.

If you want more information about what kinds of medications are in development, contact the organizations listed in the back of this book. They may know what drugs are currently being tested in the United States or used in other countries.

Although you may sometimes feel alone, you are not. Asthma affects millions of people, each of whom can learn to live healthy, active, productive lives.

Glossary

aerosol A spray.

allergens Substances that cause an allergic reaction.

alveoli The smallest parts of the lungs (the air sacs) where the exchange of oxygen and carbon dioxide takes place.

antihistamines Medications that counteract the effects of the chemical histamine in the nasal passage.

bronchial spasms Contractions of the bronchial muscles.

bronchial tubes Larger airways in the lungs.

bronchioles Smaller airways branching off from the bronchial tubes.

bronchodilators Drugs, such as albuterol, that help to open up the airways.

constrict To become narrow.

dilate To become wide.

expulsion The act of forcing out or being forced out.

hyperventilation Rapid, shallow breathing, leading to tingling sensation and oxygen loss.

immunotherapy Treatment of allergies by injecting small amounts of allergens into a patient to reduce sensitivity.

noncompliance Refusal to do something as instructed.

OTC (over-the-counter) Drugs that can be bought without a prescription from a doctor.

pulmonary disease Disease of the lungs, such as bronchitis or emphysema.

respiratory tract Airways from nose to mouth, down the trachea and through the lungs to the alveoli in the lungs.

status asthmaticus Life-threatening asthma attack.

trachea The windpipe.

Where to Go for Help

Allergy and Asthma Network/Mothers of Asthmatics, Inc.
3554 Chain Bridge Road, Suite 200
Fairfax, VA 22030-2709
(800) 878-4403
Web Site: http://www.podi.com

American Academy of Allergy and Immunology
611 East Wells Street
Milwaukee, WI 53202-3889
(414) 272-6071
Web site: http://www.aaaai.org

American Lung Association
1740 Broadway
New York, NY 10019
(800) LUNG-USA
Web site: http://www.lungusa.org

Asthma and Allergy Foundation of America (AAFA)
1125 Fifteenth Street, NW
Washington, DC 20005
(800) 7-ASTHMA
e-mail: info@aafa.org
Web site: http://www.aafa.org

**National Jewish Center for Immunology and
Respiratory Medicine**
(800) 222-LUNG

IN CANADA

Allergy/Asthma Information Association
20 South Road
Doaktown, New Brunswick E0C 1G0
(506) 362-4501

For Further Reading

Haas, Dr. Francois, and Dr. Sheila S. Haas. *The Essential Asthma Book*. New York: Charles Scribner's Sons, 1987.

Hannaway, Paul. *The Asthma Self-Help Book*. Rocklin, CA: Prima Publishing, 1992.

Paul, Glennon H., and Barbara Fufoglia. *All About Asthma and How to Live with It*. New York: Sterling Publishing Corp., Inc., 1988.

Simpson, Carolyn. *Coping with Asthma*. New York: Rosen Publishing Group, Inc., 1994.

Subak-Sharp, Gennel. *Breathing Easy: A Handbook for Asthmatics*. New York: Doubleday, 1988.

Weinstein, Allan. *Asthma*. New York: McGraw-Hill Book Co., 1987.

Young, Stuart H., Susan Shulman, and Martin Shulman. *The Asthma Handbook: A Complete Guide for Patients and Their Families*. New York: Bantam Books, 1989.

Index

A
Accolate, 30
adrenaline (epinephrine), 29–30, 36, 42
albuterol, 29
allergens, 17–20, 25, 36, 49, 57
allergies, 9, 12, 17–20, 23, 25, 36
allergy shots (immunotherapy) 36, 49
alveoli, 11
antibodies, 17
antigens, 17
antihistamines, 39

B
basophils (white blood cells), 17
B cells, 16–17
blood vessels, 11–12, 28
Brethaire, 30
bronchial spasms, 28, 50
bronchial tubes, 11–12, 17, 19, 28–30, 32, 39–42, 50
bronchioles, 11–12, 41
bronchodilating medications, 25, 27, 29–30, 34–35, 41–42

C
caffeine, 28
cats, 19–20, 50
cockroaches, 19–20
constriction, 12, 30, 42
corticosteroids, 35–36

cortisone, 35
coughing, 14, 18, 39, 44
cromolyn sodium, 29, 34

D
dander, 17, 19–20
dilation, 12, 27, 30
dust, 19–20, 49–50

E
emergency room treatment, 41–42
exercise, 21–22, 24, 27, 34, 48

F
food, 17, 19–21
Food and Drug Administration (FDA), 30, 55

G
genes, 16, 55
guilt, feelings of, 52–53

H
histamine, 17–20, 27, 29, 35
hyperventilation, 14

I
IgE (Immunoglobulin E) 17, 36
immune system, 16–17
inhalers, 7, 13–14, 19, 30–34, 39, 41, 44–46, 48–49

About the Author

Carolyn Simpson is a writer and a therapist living in Tulsa, Oklahoma. She has also written *Coping with Asthma*.

Ms. Simpson teaches psychology at Tulsa Community College.

Photo Credits

Cover and all photos by Ira Fox.